The Complete
Coffee
Book

A Gourmet Guide
to Buying, Brewing
and Cooking

by Sara Perry

photography by Edward Gowans

CHRONICLE BOOKS

Printed in Hong Kong

Library of Congress Cataloging-in-Publication Data

Perry, Sara.
    The complete coffee book: a gourmet guide to
buying, brewing, and cooking / Sara Perry,
Edward Gowans, and Judith Ann Rose.
        p.   cm.
    Includes index.
    ISBN 0-87701-899-5 [hardcover]
    ISBN 0-87701-820-0
    1. Coffee. 2. Cookery (Coffee) I. Gowans,
Edward.
II. Rose, Judith Ann. III. Title
TX817.C6P47   1991
641.6'373—dc20
90-29132 CIP

Distributed in Canada by Raincoast Books,
112 East Third Avenue, Vancouver, B.C. V5T 1C8

10 9 8 7 6 5 4 3

Chronicle Books
275 Fifth Street
San Francisco, CA 94103

To Pete, my favorite coffee companion. And to Matthew
and Julie, who have proved as stimulating as caffeine.

Design and production by Judith Rose

Editing by Catherine Gleason

Food styling by Carol Ladd

Props by Carol Ladd and Nancy Lichtwardt

Recipe testing by Shirley Jollymore

Typesetting by Irish Setter

CONTENTS

5   INTRODUCTION

7   HISTORY

11 The BEAN

17 The ROAST

25 The BREW

45 RECIPES

    46 DRINKS

    62 SAVORIES

    75 DESSERTS

94 INDEX

96 ACKNOWLEDGMENTS

INTRODUCTION

I was six when my mother's best friend Gracie came to visit us in Los Angeles and I was allowed to open the bright red tin of Hills Bros. Coffee. I knew it must be something good. There was an exotic-looking man in a flowing yellow robe and white turban on the outside of the can, and he appeared quite mysterious sipping his drink. The whoosh of aroma as I opened the lid told me this was something I wanted to try. Convincing my mother to let me have a cup, I sat at the kitchen table, feeling quite grown-up, holding a china cup brimming with hot milk, sugar, and a touch of black coffee, and listening to my mother and Gracie talk. It was heaven.

Coffee has long been one of life's subtle pleasures. Few beverages are as satisfying, comforting, or stimulating as a steaming cup, freshly brewed. Whether you enjoy it along with the morning paper, pass it out at a tense business meeting, or share it with your sweetheart after an intimate meal, a cup of coffee does more than satisfy your thirst, as hundreds of millions of coffee drinkers around the world attest.

So follow me inside coffee's history and mystique and watch the modest bean as it metamorphoses from cherry to brew. Learn to distinguish once and for all among the confusing labels that make choosing coffee a chore. Discover the fine points of the different methods of making it. Treat yourself to a range of seasonal and cultural recipes that capture coffee's essence. But first, brew yourself a cup and sit down to enjoy this book.

The HISTORY

Coffee's origins are lost in legend, but a frequently told story attributes the discovery to a herd of tired, hungry goats and their curious Ethiopian caretaker, Kaldi, in the sixth century. Weary of searching for greener pastures and eager to eat, Kaldi's herd resorted to nibbling sweet red berries off strange bushes. Unusual behavior soon followed. Old billy goats began to kick up their heels with an exuberance the prancing nannies found quite appealing. When Kaldi, witnessing this phenomenal change, tried the berries, he was soon cavorting across the hillside himself, and when he confided his discovery of the divine berries to a monk, the news was heralded at the nearby monastery. Evening prayers suddenly became more pleasant, and the glories of the heavenly berries spread.

Until the tenth century, coffee was considered a food. Ethiopian tribesmen mixed wild berries with animal fat, rolled them into balls, and ate them during their nomadic journeys. (Later, they crushed the berries and fermented them into wine.) By the thirteenth century, coffee's restorative powers were well documented in the Islamic world. It was considered a potent medicine, as well as a religious potion that helped keep the faithful awake during lengthy prayers. Islamic pilgrims spread coffee's virtues throughout the Middle East and by the end of the fifteenth century, coffeehouses supplanted neighborhood mosques as favored meeting places.

To maintain tight control of their profitable coffee trade, Arab traders sold only boiled or roasted beans. Coffee beans that could germinate and grow into fruit-bearing coffee plants were not allowed out of Arabia. It was not until the early seventeenth century that a Moslem pilgrim smuggled the first fertile beans into India. Baba Budan was reputedly the fellow who snatched seven seeds and tied them around his waist before continuing his holy pilgrimage to Mecca. When he returned home, he planted the seeds and nurtured his prolific bushes. The enterprising Dutch soon arrived at his doorstep and convinced him to part with some of his young trees, and within a few years dozens of countries were cultivating these supreme beans.

Venetian traders were the first to bring Arabian beans to Europe. The Christian world was skeptical about the pagan brew, and Pope Clement VII decided it required papal review. After one sip, His Holiness knew this drink was worthy of baptism. Sanctified, coffee no longer required an apothecary's prescription. Instead, it became the social beverage of Europe's middle class and was hawked alongside lemonade on every street corner.

In 1637, the first European coffeehouse opened in England, and within thirty years coffeehouses had replaced taverns as the island's social, commercial, and political melting pots. They were called "penny universities"—places where anything might be discussed and learned for the price of a cup of coffee. Men with similar interests frequented specific establishments, and a number of newspapers, banks, and insurance houses sprang to life around crowded wooden tables among the heady aromas of roasted beans. Lloyd's of London, today a famous insurance company, began at Edward Lloyd's coffeehouse, a place where sea merchants and underwriters gathered to talk and do business.

As the seventeenth century's preferred locale for male networking, English coffeehouses excluded females. In 1674, unhappy wives published *A Women's Petition Against Coffee*, declaring it was unhealthy for men to be spending so much time away from their homes. A year later, King Charles II tried to shut down establishments brewing beans, but he was unsuccessful, and for the next quarter century English coffeehouses continued to be male bastions. Then, during the eighteenth century, the middle class began moving back into neighborhood taverns, and London coffeehouses evolved into select clubs. Tea became a popular beverage not only at Court but among commoners, because this was a drink women and men could enjoy together, while improving trade between the British East India Trading Company and India's tea producers.

Coffeehouses declined in England, but they continued to be popular gathering places throughout Italy, Germany, France, and other

European countries. One favorite Parisian haunt was the Café Procope, which opened its doors as a coffeehouse in 1689 and over the years welcomed philosophers such as Rousseau and Voltaire (who supposedly consumed forty cups of coffee each day) and the future emperor of France, young Napoleon Bonaparte. Today, Café Procope remains a lively meeting place.

Tea was the beverage of choice for most American colonists until Boston threw its great tea party. The Dutch had introduced coffee in 1660 and served it in coffeehouses fashioned after the English model. These became the rendezvous for revolutionary activities against King George of England and his tea tax, as customers such as John Adams and Paul Revere brewed a potent cup of coffee and politics. The boycott of tea, the Boston Tea Party in 1773, and the fight for freedom established coffee as the traditional democratic drink of Americans.

Over the next two hundred years, coffee became popular around the world. Served hot or cold, it became a staple, the beverage of choice in the morning, in the evening, at lunch. In the United States alone, an estimated forty-five million cups are brewed every day.

HOW MUCH FOR A POUND? In 1683, William Penn, the founder of Pennsylvania, purchased a pound of coffee in New York for $4.68.

Three hundred years later, a pound of house-blended coffee at Dean & DeLuca in New York costs $6.50.

The BEAN

Most plants first bloom, then bear fruit. The small, shrublike coffee tree does both at once, blooming with jasmine-scented white flowers at the same time that it bears ripe and unripe fruit. This odd natural quirk makes growing coffee extremely labor intensive. On plantations where quality coffee is grown, each picker must return to the same tree several times a year to handpick only the ripe, crimson berries.

Your coffee's rich, dark brew begins with two seeds growing inside the coffee tree's fruit, or "cherry." Resembling a cranberry in size and shape, the cherry has a sweet pulp and two flat-sided seeds. These seeds are protected by a silky opaque covering, called the silverskin, and a parchment-like husk. (When only one round bean develops inside the cherry, it is called a peaberry.)

A healthy coffee tree produces five pounds of green beans a year, or about two thousand handpicked beans. Of these, perhaps four hundred beans are top quality, plucked over the course of a season with painstaking work. Compared to this, your purchase of a pound of coffee is a rather effortless task.

Tolerant, easy to please, coffee trees grow in almost any soil, but thrive in areas rich with volcanic minerals. In the seventeenth century, wild coffee trees from the highlands of Ethiopia were transported to the tropics. Today, they flourish as cultivated plants. The rainy season nurtures their growth, the sun ripens their fruit, and their beans at these lower altitudes mature in two to three months.

Although there are many species of coffee trees, only one produces exceptional coffee. *Coffea arabica*, which was first found growing in Yemen centuries ago, is the sole species of quality beans. The most widely cultivated coffee plant, arabica thrives at higher altitudes, where its beans mature slowly and have time to develop body and density. At these higher altitudes, they may take six or seven months, but this slower rate of fruit maturation gives the beans more time to develop flavor. Slower-maturing, high-density arabica beans are referred to as hard beans.

Coffea robusta is the type you are most likely to drink when you follow instructions to "add hot water and stir." Discovered in Africa toward the end of the nineteenth century, robusta is relatively new to the coffee industry but its role is significant. Because of its hardiness, high yield, and ability to grow at lower altitudes, its beans are cheaper to produce. This makes them ideal for blending with arabicas and for use in instant coffee. For those who like caffeine, robustas have twice as much kick as arabicas. Alas, their flavor tends to be harsh and pungent.

Depending on the type of coffee you drink, your beans have traveled from a very different part of the world and have been processed in one of two very different ways. One process is called dry; the other is called wet.

The **dry method** is the oldest and most natural. It is also the cheapest. The fruit either dries on the tree, or the tree is shaken or stripped and its ripe and unripe fruit spread out to dry and shrivel in the sun. Workers rake the beans several times during a two- to three-week period to make sure they dry evenly, put them through a milling machine to separate the debris from the beans, then grade them and ship them off to roasters.

In certain countries where inferior harvesting methods are practiced, and trees are shaken or stripped instead of handpicked, underdeveloped or imperfect beans are collected along with ripe ones. This not only creates inferior coffee, it also injures the trees. Most inferior coffees are processed using the dry method, but there are high-quality coffees processed dry in areas where water is scarce. Indonesian and Ethiopian coffees are two examples.

The **wet method** is used with handpicked, fully ripe, quality beans. These are the washed beans carried by specialty stores. The beans are steeped and allowed to ferment for up to twenty-four hours in large tanks. Water is gently sprayed over them to remove the pulp and any debris. Then they are dried in the sun on large patios or in commercial tumble dryers. Finally, a hulling machine removes the protective silverskin that adheres to the bean's surface, and men and women patiently grade them by size, shape, and quality, pack them in 60-

kilogram (approximately 132-pound) bags, and ship them to roasters around the world. Eventually, their long journey ends in the home of a coffee drinker like you.

NAME YOUR BEAN. When you buy coffee, you are confronted with exotic names that either indicate the country of origin or how long the bean was roasted.

Arabica beans are identified by their geographical origin. Pure and unblended, they possess the characteristic flavor and aroma of their native soil. Further geographical appellations name the district, plantation, or port from which the beans were shipped. A coffee labeled Ethiopian Harrar tells you these beans were grown near the city of Harrar in Ethiopia.

Names such as French, Viennese, and Italian refer to the amount of roasting the beans received. They are the darkest beans and they have been roasted the longest time. The beans themselves come from different countries and are usually blended to give the best each country has to offer. A Viennese Mexican tells you pure Mexican beans were roasted longer than usual. The next chapter tells you how to distinguish between roasts.

Retailers also mix and name their own blends. These names have little to do with bean content but relate to the seller's personal preferences. Alaska has yet to grow a coffee bean, but Yukon Blend is a popular Northwest coffee. If you find yourself floundering in a sea of roasts, blends, and beans, find a retailer who posts written descriptions or provides free taste samples.

PURE, UNBLENDED COFFEES FROM AROUND THE WORLD

TASTING TERMINOLOGY

ACIDITY is the sharp, snappy taste that wakes your coffee up. It has nothing to do with bitter, unpleasant sensations or your coffee's pH.

AROMA is fragrance. Your nose is the first judge of the flavors released from the bean and will tell you a great deal about your coffee's freshness and personality.

BRAZIL: Over 30 percent of the world's coffee is produced in Brazil. Most is used in the production of canned and instant coffee. If you enjoy a mildly acidic, medium-bodied coffee, **Bourbon Santos** makes a fine brew.

COLOMBIA: Second to Brazil in worldwide production, Colombia's crop is all handpicked, washed arabica beans. **Medellín**, Colombia's most famous coffee, sings with a rich, finely balanced flavor.

COSTA RICA: All of the beans from this Central American country are washed arabicas. Possessing a rich, full body, they tingle with acidity.

DOMINICAN REPUBLIC: Over 80 percent of the coffee grown here heads to the United States. Known as **Santo Domingo**, it is moderately acid, pleasant, without a pungent personality.

ECUADOR: Some of the highest-altitude coffee plantations in the world perch on the mountains of this South American country, but the coffee they produce is indifferent and most often used for blends.

ETHIOPIA: According to legend, coffee's name came from the Ethiopian region of Kaffa. **Ethiopian Harrar** is one of the world's best-known, strongest-flavored coffees. Its rich, thick flavor caresses your tongue like a fine Burgundy.

GUATEMALA: The midland mountain regions of this Central American country nurture aromatic, mellow-bodied coffees. Grown in the regions of **Antigua** and **Coban**, these beans have a smoky, acidic flavor that many people feel makes the perfect cup of coffee.

HAITI: Frequently used in blends and dark roasts, the beans of this Caribbean country are very popular in Europe, where coffee drinkers appreciate a mellow taste that has a touch of sweetness.

HAWAII: This is the only place in the United States with an ideal climate for growing coffee. The **Kona** district boasts the highest yield per tree in the world and produces an aromatic, mellow-bodied coffee.

INDIA: Mysore is the most well known of the Indian coffees. It is a dark coffee, soft and delicate as a flower on the tongue.

INDONESIA: Named after the islands where they are grown, **Sumatra**, **Celebes**, and **Java** coffees are famous for their rich, spicy, full-bodied flavor.

JAMAICA: Blue Mountain is like a beautiful woman who is talked about everywhere but seldom seen. Aromatic, sweet, and extremely mellow, it seldom reaches the United States, as most of the crop goes to Japan.

KENYA: This African coffee has a delicate smoothness and winey aftertaste that is popular in both Great Britain and the United States.

MEXICO: The best-known coffees are the **Coatepec**, **Pluma**, and **Oaxaca**. With a full, acidic body and a fragrant aroma, they are very popular for blending.

PERU: The **Chanchamayo** Valley is home to a subtly flavored, lightly acidic coffee.

TANZANIA: Rich and full-bodied, the arabica beans of this African nation are grown in mountainous areas. The best known flourish on the slopes of Mount Kilimanjaro.

VENEZUELA: Here, the coffee industry is declining due to the upwelling of petroleum interests. **Mérida** is the light-bodied, sweet coffee from Maracaibo. It is often used in blends but is excellent served pure.

YEMEN: Mocha, named after the ancient Arabian port of Moka on the Red Sea, is a fragrant, creamy brew with a rich almost chocolaty aftertaste. Shop carefully for this bean and be aware that genuine Mocha beans are rare.

BODY is the heaviness and thickness of a coffee as it touches your tongue. Remember how a hearty red wine slides down your throat, and a white glides. In the same way, a rich Sumatran and a mild Mexican coffee give you different weight sensations.

FLAVOR: Defining flavor is a little like defining love. It's all in the relationship. Flavor is really a combination of acidity, aroma, and body. In some cases one quality stands out, for instance, the singular tang of a Costa Rican. In others, like the full-flavored Sumatran, a broader range of qualities is celebrated.

Although tribesmen munched crushed coffee beans and animal fat as a trail staple, it was not until the thirteenth century that the secrets of roasted coffee were discovered. Unlike fragrant wine grapes or scented tea leaves, raw coffee beans conceal their flavor. It is only with roasting that flavors and aromas are liberated.

Raw beans store indefinitely, but the roasted bean must be used quickly. So, up to the mid-nineteenth century, coffee drinkers and local shopkeepers roasted their beans over an open fire or in an oven in small batches. It was only after demand became concentrated in urban centers, where distribution time was short, that large-scale roasting became practical.

The principle of roasting coffee is simple: heat raw beans between 380° and 480° F. Complexity and skill enter the equation because each variety of bean has its own ideal roasting time. The experienced roastmaster must know his beans and adjust temperature and roasting time according to sight and aroma.

Most roasting machines resemble clothes dryers. A revolving cylinder allows beans to roast uniformly. The heat inside the cylinder draws off moisture so the volatile aromatic oils can emerge. These oils give coffee its flavor and aroma.

As the beans roast, distinct stages of appearance and flavor occur. Although roasters have identified these stages, they have a hard time agreeing what to call each one. A Full Roast in one store may be called Viennese in another. This is when you hope there is a knowledgeable person or a descriptive card close by. After the beans have reached the desired roast, they are quickly cooled to avoid over-cooking. Air jets are used for higher-quality beans. This is referred to as a **dry roast**. In contrast, large-scale commercial roasters frequently cool their beans with water jets, which tend to swell the beans with unwanted moisture. Naturally, this is referred to as a **wet roast**.

Although many commercial enterprises continue to roast their beans in small batches under the watchful eye and nose of a roastmaster, computerized roasting machines have crept into the marketplace.

The aroma of roasting coffee has not been without its dangers. In the late 1700s, Prussia's Frederick the Great banned the consumption of coffee by ordinary citizens. Forceful and prejudiced, he wanted his people to drink the beverage of their fatherland, beer, and he hired retired soldiers as coffee smellers to arrest anyone secretly roasting coffee or brewing a cup. Frederick also encouraged physicians to report that coffee drinking caused sterility. This generated a famous musical protest: Bach's "Coffee Cantata." Bach, a lover of coffee, was the father of twenty children.

ROASTING STAGES

LIGHT or **PALE ROAST** *is the typical roast used for canned or institutional coffee, but it is also used for delicately flavored beans. In both cases, the beans have a dry, cinnamon-colored surface and are often brewed as a morning coffee and served with milk.*

MEDIUM, CITY, or **AMERICAN ROAST** *is the all-purpose roast most Americans seem to prefer. The beans are medium brown in color, and their surface is dry. Although this brew may have snappy, acidic qualities, its flavor tends to be flat.*

Roasting times have been cut to a minute, but in the opinion of many coffee lovers, the subtle nuances produced by the roastmaster have been lost.

If you want the satisfaction of the ultimate fresh brew, join the ranks of the **home roasters**. A number of small home roasting devices are available, from stovetop models resembling old-fashioned popcorn poppers to small electric roasters manufactured by Melitta and Sirocco. You will find that the most difficult aspect of home roasting is not the time, technique, or mess but the availability of good unroasted green beans. If you decide to experiment, try Colombian beans. They seem to offer novices the best results. And remember that darker does not mean stronger. The darker roasts may have a more pronounced taste, but the amount of caffeine in your brew depends on the amount of soluble oils left in the beans. Due to their longer roasting times and greater loss of soluble oils, darker roasts have less caffeine than the lighter varieties.

STORING YOUR BEANS: Your coffee beans' worst enemies are air and moisture. Once your beans are exposed to these vagrants, the flavorful oils vanish like New Year's resolutions.

One way you can postpone their deterioration is to buy and store your beans whole. Another way to prevent flavor loss is to store loose beans in an airtight container that will hold all of them without leaving a large air space. You don't want to use the one-pound bag you bring home from the store or a leftover yogurt container. You do want a glass or ceramic jar whose lid has a rubber gasket to assure an airtight closure.

Keep any vacuum-packed beans sealed until you are ready to use them. Correctly stored in a cool, dry place, whole beans will retain their flavor for up to three weeks after roasting. Some experts suggest refrigerating unused beans, but this is not necessary. In fact, every time you take the container out of the refrigerator, unwanted condensation collects inside. So, if you do tempt fate by purchasing more than a two-weeks' supply of coffee at one time, store the remainder in the freezer. Packaged in freezer bags or airtight containers, beans will keep for several months. (It helps to divide them into amounts you can pull out and use within two weeks.)

Since freshly roasted beans give off carbon dioxide, canned coffees are pre-staled to avoid an exploding coffee can. No coffee lover wants stale coffee, so many specialty-coffee roasters now pack their whole and ground beans in a vacuum container with a one-way valve. This keeps the staling process at bay by releasing carbon dioxide without admitting moisture and oxygen.

The very best way to tell if your beans are fresh is to use your nose. Smell them. A sweet, earthy, coffee aroma is what you want. If they have a dull, lifeless odor, put the beans back and find another store.

GRINDING YOUR OWN: It takes so little time and the reward is so great. Grinding your own beans is the most significant thing you can do to improve the taste of your coffee. Ground beans will lose their vitality within a week. Grinding your own cuts down on the time aromatic oils are exposed to air. Before your beans' flavor is lost, you will be delighting in a freshly brewed cup.

Once you decide to buy a grinder, there are basically three types from which you can choose: the mortar and pestle, the hand mill, and the electric grinder.

For centuries, coffee drinkers used a **mortar and pestle** to grind their beans. You will find it time-consuming and, unless you are an expert, you'll produce an uneven grind.

An old-fashioned alternative is a **hand mill**. Based on the same principle as a millstone, invented by the Turks in the fifteenth century to grind flour, hand mills come in two basic designs: a box or lap grinder and a wall-mounted version reminiscent of a fancy meat grinder. You grind the beans by feeding them into the top of the box. A funnel or slotted screw drops the beans between two corrugated steel discs, one stationary, one rotated by a crank. When you turn the crank,

FULL, HIGH, or VIENNESE ROAST is the favorite of many specialty-coffee stores because the taste strikes an even balance between sweetness and sharpness. The beans are chestnut brown in color and show patches of oil. French, Continental, or Dark Roast has a tangy, rich flavor. The beans are the color of semisweet chocolate and shiny with oil. Add chicory to this roast to make a Louisiana-style coffee.

ESPRESSO or ITALIAN ROAST is the darkest of all roasts. Its almost-black beans have a shiny, oily surface. All acidic qualities and specific coffee flavors are gone, but its pungent flavor is a favorite of espresso lovers.

COFFEE GRINDS

COARSE: *This grind's large granules are suitable for the jug or plunger method. A coarse grind is also used in the pumping percolator, which has large filter holes.*

MEDIUM: *This grind resembles sugar granules and is used primarily with vacuum and flat-bottom drip makers. It is the most versatile grind and suits all brewing methods except espresso and Turkish.*

FINE/ESPRESSO: *With a texture like cornmeal, this grind works well with drip and filter brewing methods. It is also used with espresso machines and the Neapolitan flip-drip.*

PULVERIZED: *Employed exclusively for Turkish coffee, this grind is as fine as flour. Most home grinders cannot get beans this fine. Ask your coffee merchant to grind it for you or buy a special Turkish grinder.*

the beans are crushed between the two discs and fall into a drawer at the bottom of the grinder. You determine the fineness of the grind by adjusting the space between the discs. Electric coffee mills duplicate the action of the hand mill and give you a uniform grind at the touch of a button. Costlier than other methods, they can also be more difficult to clean.

Unsurprisingly, **electric grinders** owe their popularity to ease of handling. Working much like your kitchen blender, with a central stainless steel blade rotating at high speed, electric grinders repeatedly chop your beans into tiny pieces. Your grind's fineness is determined by the length of time you run the blade. The only disadvantage is this grinder's tendency to overheat the beans, so that flavor is lavished on the air rather than your cup.

Keep in mind that the way you grind your beans depends in part on the brewing method you use. The next chapter gives you details about the most popular brewing methods and their special requirements.

CAFFEINE IN COFFEE: If you find that your after-dinner demitasse keeps you awake or that office coffee gives you the jitters, caffeine may be the reason. Occurring naturally in many plants (coffee, tea, and cocoa to name a few) caffeine is a mildly habit-forming drug whose side effects have become a popular health issue in our culture. Controversial investigations have claimed that ingesting caffeine may lead to cancer, fibrocystic disease, heart attacks, and sterility, but there is no hard medical evidence that conclusively proves these allegations.

If you are trying to cut down on caffeine, but still want the pleasurable taste of coffee, there are some alternatives. The first may surprise you.

Robusta and arabica differ in the amount of caffeine they bring to a cup of coffee. Robusta, used primarily for canned and instant coffee, contains 2.5 percent caffeine; arabica contains only 1 percent. One

Coffee grinders come in an array of shapes and sizes to suit your coffee needs and stylistic preferences.

answer to coffee jitters is to check your office coffee supply. If it comes in a can, dump it and replace it with less-stimulating arabica beans. The other alternative is to switch to decaf.

If you do decide to cut down on the amount of caffeine you drink, you may experience some minor withdrawal symptoms—headache, drowsiness, even nausea. Don't worry, it's normal and will go away after a day or two.

DECAFFEINATED COFFEE: One-quarter of all the coffee drinkers in the United States drink decaffeinated coffee. During the past two decades, the techniques for removing caffeine have improved dramatically, giving us a rich, full-bodied brew. There are basically two ways of extracting caffeine: one method is direct; the other is indirect. Neither produces any measurable health risks.

Caffeine is eliminated from the unroasted bean by a water or solvent process. In both instances, caffeine is brought to the surface by treating the green bean with warm water and steam. In the **indirect method**, the unroasted bean is soaked in a water solution, which removes caffeine along with other water-soluble components. In a separate step, this mixture is filtered through activated charcoal (the Swiss water process) or through a solvent, and the caffeine is segregated.

In the **direct method**, the softened bean is treated with a solvent (methylene chloride), which binds with the caffeine and is then rinsed or evaporated away. It is a faster, perhaps superior method because it disturbs fewer of coffee's desirable components. However, one frequently raised concern is the possibility that residual chloride may be left on the roasted bean and consumed by the coffee drinker. You will be happy to know this is close to impossible as the temperature for roasting coffee is 450° F, and methylene chloride evaporates at 170° F.

There are variations to each of these procedures, and it can be fascinating talking to your coffee merchant about the different methods. He will be one of the first to know of any significant changes in the decaffeinating process.

COFFEE ADDITIVES: An incredible array of nuts, cereals, and vegetables have been tried at one time or another to extend or replace coffee. When coffee supplies became scarce during the Civil War, desperate Confederate soldiers used roasted sweet potato and Indian corn as a substitute. While the incentive for a coffee substitute or a coffee extender is often economy, the motive for flavoring is to improve an inferior brew or to create a fashionable new taste. Two popular extenders that are also taste enhancers are chicory and fig.

Many believe chicory is an exotic herb blended into the dark-roasted coffees of French, Cajun, and Vietnamese cuisine. Actually, it's the root of a plant related to our dandelion, whose young leaves make a great endive salad. Roasted chicory root has a peppery sharpness that gives even the darkest roasts a distinctive taste. Far from being rare, chicory is cheaper than coffee and its unique flavor is often used to conceal the unsavory characteristics of commercially marketed robusta beans. Unlike the pungent aftertaste of chicory, roasted fig imparts a delicate, fruity flavor to coffee. It is a popular blend in the United Kingdom, but is scarce in the United States.

*To the purist, **flavored coffees** and wine coolers are kissing cousins. Many traditionally minded coffee drinkers believe that coffee's complex nature should be left alone, but the latest trend is toward flavored coffees. For best results, flavoring is added to freshly roasted beans while they are still warm and will absorb the additive easily. Chocolate, Amaretto, Irish Cream, French Vanilla —take your pick from these and a score of others.*

The BREW

There is nothing magical about brewing coffee. It's the same basic process whether you plunk an inexpensive tin cup over a camp fire or plug in an elaborate electric espresso machine. You simply pour hot water over ground coffee long enough to extract the oils and gases that will make the water taste good. All you really need, in addition to your beans, is a container for the water and, in most cases, a source of heat.

For over three hundred years, people have been inventing all kinds of gadgets to do this simple task. The most popular methods and tools and a few of the most eccentric are described later in this chapter, but no matter which you choose, a few guidelines, described in more detail in the following pages, will help you brew the best possible cup of coffee.

- MAKE SURE YOUR EQUIPMENT IS CLEAN.
- USE WATER THAT TASTES GOOD.
- BREW COFFEE AT THE CORRECT WATER TEMPERATURE.
- USE THE CORRECT GRIND AND BREWING TIME.
- USE THE CORRECT AMOUNT OF COFFEE.
- SERVE IT FRESH.

MAKE SURE YOUR EQUIPMENT IS CLEAN. Remember the smell of the office coffeepot you finally decided to clean? Or the first time you uncorked the picnic basket thermos last summer? Coffee contains oil. Every time you brew a pot, some of the residual oil is left on your container. If the oil in your coffeepot is not removed, it will mar every fresh pot you brew, making it taste rancid and bitter.

So, clean your pot thoroughly after each use, but don't use soap or detergent. They leave a film that will transform your Guatemalan Antigua into a perfumed imposter. Rinse the pot with hot water and scrub it with a non-abrasive sponge, or use a little baking soda. Anytime you use an abrasive brush or cleaner, you will scratch the interior surface of your pot. Those scratches trap unpleasant coffee oils and mineral deposits. (This is especially true with metal coffeepots. Porcelain and glass pots are less susceptible.) After you've washed your pot, be sure to dry it. You might also want to rinse and dry your kettle to help prevent the buildup of mineral deposits.

USE WATER THAT TASTES GOOD. If the water flowing out of your kitchen faucet reminds you of a cool, crystal-clear mountain spring, it will make a great cup of coffee. Coffee is 99 percent water. When your water tastes bad, your coffee tastes worse.

If you use tap water, make sure it is cold and let it run a moment before filling your kettle. Warm tap water has a flat taste from lying in the hot-water tank. This is also true of cold water when it sits overnight in your water pipes. If you don't like the taste of your tap water, experiment with different filtered or bottled waters until you find one whose taste you enjoy.

BREW COFFEE AT THE CORRECT WATER TEMPERATURE. The real reason you use hot water to brew your coffee is to draw out the flavor. You don't want to cook the beans. That was done during the roasting process. The best brewing temperature for coffee is between 200° F and 205° F, just below water's boiling point of 212° F. When your kettle has reached a rapid boil, lift it off the burner and hold it for a moment before pouring the water over your grounds. That will lower your water to the correct temperature. If you leave your kettle boiling on the stove too long, the water will lose too much oxygen and your cup of coffee will taste dull. If you use an automatic coffeemaker, remember that its thermostat has been set to brew with cold water.

USE THE CORRECT GRIND AND BREWING TIME. To make a great cup of coffee you have to get 19 percent of the weight of the coffee grounds into your finished brew. This may sound difficult, but you will find it is easy. It just takes a bit of experimenting, and maybe some reading in your coffeepot's instruction manual. Two tips on grind may help. Number one, don't grind your beans so fine that the particles clog your filter. Number two, don't grind so coarse that the hot water rushes through the grounds without having a chance to really wet them and draw out their flavors. The finer your grind, the more surface area there is and the more easily hot water can extract the aromatic oils.

With a fine grind, your brewing cycle should take no longer than four minutes; with a drip grind, 4 to 6 minutes; with a regular grind, no more that 8 minutes. Remember that brewing coffee too long will give it an unpleasant, bitter taste.

USE THE CORRECT AMOUNT OF COFFEE. To make a full-flavored cup of coffee, use 2 level tablespoons of coffee (or 1 Approved Coffee Measure) to 6 ounces of water. Keep in mind that 6 ounces will fill a normal cup, but not a large mug. If you prefer stronger coffee, use more grounds. If you like a weaker brew, dilute your regular-strength coffee with hot water. Don't use less coffee because that will lead to over-extraction and a bitter cup.

SERVE IT FRESH. The aroma and clean taste of that first cup you brew in the morning is a far cry from the mid-morning coffee you zap in the microwave. Within 15 minutes of brewing, coffee begins to deteriorate. Its aromatic oils start to evaporate, and its color and taste become dark and flat.

Preserving that first delicious brew is a challenge. The best way is to store your coffee in a preheated, vacuum-insulated thermos bottle. Many types and sizes are available, from fluted French flasks to sleek, stainless steel Japanese canisters. You can also keep your freshly brewed coffee in a warm-water bath or on a heating element no warmer than 190° F. This method works well for an hour. After that, you may notice a change in flavor.

Finally, never reuse coffee grounds. It is like revisiting a past lover: everything that was great has already been savored.

PLUNGER

COLD-WATER CONCENTRATE: *A popular way to make coffee is a cold-water extraction process that produces a strong concentrate. It's useful because you can store it in the refrigerator and make individual cups of coffee by diluting 2 tablespoons of concentrate in 1 cup of water. The only drawback is that most of the aromatic oils brought out by hot water are not released in cold water, so this coffee tends to taste bland and generic.*
To make cold-water concentrate, soak 1 pound of coffee grounds in 8 cups of cold water for 24 hours, then filter and refrigerate. To filter, use a large bowl and a filter cone or buy a specially made brewer, such as the Toddy.

The plunger pot's twenties' design, featuring cylindrical glass and chrome architecture, makes it a perfect vessel for the nineties. It looks splendid on a breakfast tray with warmed croissants or by candlelight after a gracious dinner. Although the plunger pot's good looks and portability make it very attractive, you may not like the fact that the filtered grounds remain at the bottom of the pot. Since the grounds remain in slight contact with the water, you may find you have a stronger brew than you like. There is also the minor inconvenience of cleaning the three plunger parts. Nevertheless, devotees agree there is no better way to set a provocative atmosphere.

The pot cannot be placed directly on a heating element, so it's a good idea to preheat the plunger and pot with warm water. To brew, measure 2 level tablespoons of fine- to medium-ground coffee per cup into the glass cylinder. Pour in the correct amount of water just off the boil and stir the grounds with a spoon. This helps to assure that all the grounds are wet. Then set the plunger on top of the cylinder and allow the grounds to steep.

After 4 to 5 minutes, press the plunger slowly and steadily down. This traps the coffee grounds at the bottom of your pot. If you have selected too fine a grind, pushing down the plunger can prove to be an athletic feat. While you will find the workout well worth it, choose a coarser grind next time. Medium grind works well.

The classic French press is the elegant, sculptural Melior. Evoking outdoor cafés and intimate conversations, the metal-framed Melior remains the most popular, and costly, plunger pot. Bodum makes a less-expensive and less-romantic version that is available in brightly colored plastic frames.

NEAPOLITAN FLIP-DRIP

The elegant figure of the porcelain French Drip Pot (page 4) catches every eye. The long cylindrical neck contains a filter basket that allows water to pass through the grounds into the serving pot. Many models are made in two removable sections, the neck section and the serving pot. Others, such as the model in the photograph, are of one piece. This fragile beauty needs constant vigilance, since only a small amount of water can be added to the filter at one time, but it always makes a rich, thick cup of coffee.

In the early nineteenth century, while most Europeans and Americans were steeping their coffee in an open pot, a French tinsmith invented the double percolating coffeepot. It is composed of two metal cylinders and a filter basket that fits snugly between them. The top section, with the spout, pours. The bottom section acts as a boiler. Reminiscent of a childhood toy, the flip-drip makes a strong, rich brew that is best enjoyed in a demitasse with a sliver of lemon. Unfortunately, most macchinettas are made of aluminum and if not cleaned properly will give off a metallic taste. Also, aluminum doesn't retain heat, so you must drink your coffee promptly.

When you make what has become Italy's coffee, fill the boiler with cold water up to the tiny escape hole near the top. Insert the filter basket into the boiler and add drip-grind Italian-roast coffee until the basket is almost full and the coffee forms a mound. Screw the filter basket on top of the coffee, place the spout section over the filter, and snap it shut.

After the flip-drip has spent several minutes on medium heat, you will notice steam escaping from the hole on the side of its boiler. When it does, remove the pot and flip it over so that the top section is on the bottom. (Have some oven mitts handy in case the pot and its handles are too hot to touch.) In a few minutes, after the water has filtered through the ground coffee, you will savor a cup of coffee the citizens of Naples have adopted as their namesake.

In Italy they call it napoletana macchinetta; *in France, the* café *filtre. But its American nickname describes its unique and amusing characteristics best: the flip-drip.*

FILTER

The filter paper method is an excellent way to brew a clear, light-bodied, fragrant cup of coffee. Paper filters make it easy to discard grounds and assure a clean coffeepot. The only disadvantage to using disposable filters, besides having to periodically purchase them, is the flat papery flavor that sometimes slips into your brew. If that bothers you, a reusable gold-mesh filter, found in most specialty-coffee stores, will solve your problem.

Before you begin brewing, preheat your pot by rinsing it in hot water. Measure 2 level tablespoons of finely ground coffee per cup into your filter and place the filter basket on top of your ceramic or glass pot. Begin by pouring a small amount of water, just off the boil, over the grounds. This will help to wet the grounds and insure maximum taste. Then add the remaining water and allow it to seep through the filter. After you remove the filter basket, stir your coffee. This helps distribute the heat and flavor throughout your pot.

There are a number of automatic drip coffeemakers available for home use: Braun, Melitta, Krups, and Mr. Coffee, to name a few. They offer the convenience of electric percolators but produce a better-tasting cup of coffee. Thank goodness for Melitta's ingenuity. Otherwise, we'd be stuck with Mrs. Olson's boiled brew.

In 1908, German housewife Melitta Bentz, after trying to filter the sediment out of her husband's coffee with a linen towel, substituted a sheet of blotter paper placed over a perforated brass bowl. Today, over 80 percent of all German households use this easy, foolproof method, called the Melitta filter system.

VACUUM POT

This is quite possibly the most elegant way to brew good coffee. Suggesting a mode of life few of us have seen outside episodes of "Masterpiece Theatre," the vacuum pot creates an unhurried ceremony out of watching coffee brew.

To experience this delectable pleasure yourself, fill the bottom glass bowl with cold water and add the correct amount of medium-fine to finely ground coffee to the upper bowl, which has been fitted with a funnel and filter. Insert this precarious crucible into the lower pot, twist it to create a seal, and place the pot over your heat source. When the water boils, rises in the funnel, and spills over the coffee grounds, stir the grounds and let the brew steep.

Then, remove the pot from your heat source and watch the magic begin. The vacuum created in the lower pot draws the brewed coffee back through the filter and funnel. After several minutes, you will be ready to serve an exceptional cup of clear, flavorful coffee.

The vacuum pot may prove to be a challenge when you try to put fresh coffee grounds into the top bowl and cannot balance it because of the stem, or when you try to remove the top portion, filled with saturated hot coffee grounds, and perch it on some surface so it doesn't drip over or roll off the candlelit table. But so what if it's messy and somewhat fragile? All of us are at one time or another.

In the United States, an attractive stovetop vacuum brewer by Bodum is available in most specialty-coffee stores and comes with a stand and spirit lamp that make tabletop brewing possible. But the most elegant model, the British Cona, is the one to find. Made for a life of leisure, it works only by lamp.

An alchemist's dream, the vacuum pot was invented in 1840 by the Scottish marine scientist Robert Napier. During World War I, Americans found its gadgetry intriguing. Today, we find its brewing method nostalgic and dramatic.

MOKA EXPRESS

Espresso in Italian means "fast," and at the 1855 Paris Exposition the Edward Santais caffè espresso machine amazed visitors by making two thousand cups of coffee in one hour. Alas, the coffee was a disappointment. The steam scalded the coffee grounds and made the espresso bitter. It was not until 1946, when Achille Gaggia designed the first non-steam espresso machine, that a combination of speed and efficiency made a smooth, rich cup of espresso.

Not as highly fashioned as its festooned, copper-studded Italian relative, which inhabits noisy coffeehouses and chic bars, the simple, self-contained Moka Express makes its rich, aromatic espresso in the unruffled atmosphere of your own kitchen. The pot's smooth, heavy base works equally well on electric and gas stoves, and its moderate price makes the delights of espresso available to everyone.

The original Moka pot was made of hard aluminum, which conducts heat efficiently but can leave coffee with a metallic taste. Newer models are produced from stainless steel.

To make your espresso, unscrew the top of the Moka pot from its base, remove the filter funnel, and fill the base with cold, fresh water right up to the brass safety valve. Lightly pack the funnel with a finely ground Continental or Espresso roast and place the funnel back in the base. (The funnel has been designed to take the correct measure. If it is not filled, you will end up with an unappealing, watery brown liquid.) Firmly screw the top onto the base and place your Moka pot over medium heat.

As the water in the base begins to boil, pressure forces the water up through the grounds and extracts their rich, strong essence. When you hear a gurgling sound, you will know that all of the water has been forced through the grounds and your espresso is ready to serve.

Take the pot off the heat and pour your delicious, heavy-bodied brew in demitasse cups. Add a twist of lemon peel. Then sit down and enjoy it with the one indispensable ingredient for great espresso: an interesting companion.

A thin slice of lemon peel gives a fresh, distinctive character to espresso. Rub it gently around the rim of your demitasse before resting it on your saucer. Be wary of nonorganic lemons and wash them carefully. Pesticides do not belong in your coffee.

ESPRESSO

In addition to the stovetop espresso pot, there are many sophisticated countertop espresso machines available for home use: La Pavoni, Avanti, Gaggia, and Krups to name a few. Each creates a rich, individual cup of espresso by forcing pressurized hot water through a small filter basket filled with dark-roasted, finely ground coffee. An attractive feature on most of these machines is a cappuccino nozzle that uses the steam collected at the top of the boiler to heat and froth milk. Genteel models require a mere push of a button. The more muscular versions are equipped with a handle attached to a spring-powered piston and demand a stronger arm. Besides the high price tag attached to these machines, the problem of locating service or parts if the machine ever breaks down is worth considering before you make an investment.

A NOTE ON THE PUMPING PERCOLATOR

Many Americans grew up with the familiar sound and fragrant smell of coffee brewing in a stovetop or electric percolator. Hardware and department stores still find shelf space for the pumping percolator, but you'll be hard pressed to find one in any specialty-coffee store. At its pinnacle in the thirties, the percolator's bubbling beat gave the impression of a happy home and well-tended family. Little did we realize those sounds and smells violated the principles of brewing good coffee. The pumping percolator works by steam pressure, which continuously forces boiling water up a central tube and over the grounds. When this goes on for longer than the maximum time of eight minutes, as it often does, the brew becomes bitter. The fragrances wafting through the air are the aromas you should be enjoying in your cup.

A smaller, home version of the ornate caffè espresso machine, complete with brass eagle icon, delights old-fashioned romantics and affluent aficionados.

IBRIK

Kaimaki, *the thin, bubbly froth that appears on the just-brewed surface of Turkish coffee, is a sign of great technique. It is also a sign of good fortune if the host is able to pour some of this foam into his guest's demitasse.*

This brass or copper pot with its long narrow handle is the traditional vessel used for making rich, strong Turkish or Greek-style coffee. You can make Turkish coffee in any pot, but there is a certain mystery and romance to the ritual of brewing in the ibrik.

The method most commonly used today originated in the early sixteenth century and is unique in several ways. First, spices such as cardamom, cinnamon, and nutmeg are often ground with the coffee to add exotic flavors, and sugar is added with the coffee grounds while brewing to make a sweet, syrupy drink. Then the coffee is brought to a boil three times, not just once. In earlier times, Egyptian hosts would add a fragrant dollop of ambergris at the bottom of each cup, to allow it to impart its perfume and its powers as an aphrodisiac. Today, we stick to the more traditional method of brewing. For each demitasse, place 2 teaspoons of pulverized coffee and 1 teaspoon of granulated sugar in the ibrik. Add ¼ cup of water for each demitasse and stir to dissolve the sugar. Make sure the ibrik is only half full, because as you gently boil your brew, foam will begin to rise and double.

After the coffee has come to a boil, and the foam has reached the rim, remove your ibrik from the heat until the foam subsides. Repeat this twice and then gently pour the coffee into demitasse cups so that some of the foam tops each cup. If you are careful, most of the coffee grounds will stay in the ibrik. After your cup is filled, wait a few moments to let any grounds settle, then enjoy.

Arabian Mocha, the traditional bean used in making Turkish coffee, was named after the ancient Yemen city of Moka, which supplied all of the world's coffee until the latter part of the seventeenth century. For many years, Yemen Mocha was not available in the United States, but it is beginning to make a reappearance in many specialty-coffee stores.

OPEN POT

TREKKER'S NOTE:
Fresh, fragrant coffee made with real beans in an open pot takes no more time, energy, or room in your backpack than do those insipid instants.

Cowboy, or hobo, coffee is one of the oldest and simplest ways to brew. All you need is water, ground coffee, heat, and a container. In many countries, this open-pot method remains the most widely used.

Originally, water was boiled vigorously with the grounds, but in the eighteenth century the French discovered that steeping coffee, much the way we make a pot of tea, made a much better cup of coffee. The only trick is separating the grounds from the brew before it is served.

The easiest way is a strainer. A clean sock will do, as will any number of other ingenious devices. In England, an egg white was dropped into the coffee as it boiled. The coagulating white seized most of the floating debris. In Scandinavian countries, fish skins were employed, although, naturally, they tended to flavor the drink. The best solution is to pour a few tablespoons of cold water over the surface of your just-brewed coffee. The cold water drops, pulling the grounds to the bottom of your pot. Some buckaroos add a freshly broken egg shell with their coffee grounds to help clarify the brew.

To make cowboy coffee, you need 4 tablespoons of coarse-ground coffee for each pint of fresh water. Combine the coffee and water in a clean pot and bring just to a boil. Stir slightly to dissolve any lumps and to moisten the grounds. Remove your container from the heat, cover, and allow to steep for 5 minutes. Strain the coffee or allow the grounds to settle at the bottom of the container and serve in warmed mugs, preferably by a camp fire.

In the legendary American West, the unique aroma and taste of cowboy coffee came from a well-used pot that was never washed—perhaps to keep the memories of a hundred roundups close at hand.

RECIPES

ADVICE TO THE COOK

Coffee is the prime ingredient in dozens of delicious drinks, but it is also the secret taste enhancer of chicken, steak, shrimp, and lamb, not to mention cookies and cakes. Recipes for these and other culinary delights follow.

Each recipe designates the type and the strength of coffee you should use. Refer to "Roasting Stages" on pages 18 and 19 when a recipe requires a specific roast, and to "Coffee Grinds" on page 20 to identify specific grinds. The following list will help you to determine correct strength.

REGULAR STRENGTH: 2 level tablespoons ground coffee or 2 teaspoons instant coffee granules to each 6 ounces (¾ cup) of water.

EXTRA STRENGTH: 2 level tablespoons ground coffee or 2 teaspoons instant coffee granules to each 4 ounces (½ cup) of water.

DOUBLE STRENGTH: 4 level tablespoons ground coffee or 4 teaspoons instant coffee granules to each 6 ounces (¾ cup) of water.

ESPRESSO: 2 level tablespoons ground espresso or 2 teaspoons instant espresso granules to each 3 ounces (½ cup minus 2 tablespoons) of water.

Don't forget: In a recipe it is always best to use freshly brewed coffee made with good-tasting water and freshly ground beans. Unless you are especially concerned about caffeine, it is best to use regular beans. Decaffeinated beans tend to give a flat taste to food.

ESPRESSO

Genuine espresso is brewed under pressure in an espresso machine. A substitute can be brewed using a drip pot and filter paper. Some people appreciate the citrus taste of lemon peel rubbed around the rim of their demitasse.

In a small kettle, bring the water to a boil. Remove the kettle from the source of heat and let it rest for 30 seconds.

Meanwhile, place the filter paper in the filter cone or basket of your drip pot. Place the coffee grounds inside the filter paper and pour ½ cup of water over the grounds to wet and settle them. Add the remaining water and let it drip through the pot.

To serve, pour the espresso into 4 demitasse cups and garnish each with a lemon peel curl.

Serves 4.

1½ cups water
8 tablespoons finely ground French- or Italian-roast coffee
4 lemon peel curls for garnish

CAFÉ AU LAIT

One of the pleasures of breakfast in France is a steaming bowl of *café au lait*. In Italy it is called *caffè latte* and is made with espresso or an Italian roast. In Mexico, ask for *café con leche*.

Heat the milk to scalding using a pressurized steamer or in a small saucepan over medium heat. (If you heat the milk with a pressurized steamer, you will make your milk blissfully frothy.) Pour the hot coffee and hot milk simultaneously into 2 French *café au lait* bowls or 4 regular-sized cups.

Serves 2 to 4.

2 cups whole milk
2 cups French-roast coffee

Left to right: Espresso; Café au Lait; Cappuccino (recipe on page 49).

ICED COFFEE

The trick to perfect iced coffee is to use freshly brewed extra-strength coffee prepared no longer than 3 hours in advance. If you use yesterday's surplus or anything older than 3 hours, you'll find it has lost its flavor and tastes flat. It is also important to brew regular-strength coffee, since ice cubes made the normal way with water will dilute the drink as they melt.

    Another way around a watery drink is to use coffee ice cubes. Fresh leftover coffee can be frozen into ice cubes and used with regular-strength coffee to make a refreshing summer drink. For a special treat, a scoop of vanilla ice cream gives a wonderful contrast in flavor and color.

16 ice cubes
3 cups extra-strength coffee, cooled to room temperature

Place 4 ice cubes into each of 4 tall, chilled glasses. Pour ¾ cup of the coffee into each glass and serve.

Serves 4.

CAPPUCCINO

(Picture on page 46.)

Cappuccino is often called a divine drink. It takes its name from the Capuchins, a holy order of friars whose robes are the same color as this heavenly beverage.

2⅔ cups espresso
1⅓ cups whole milk, steamed

Authentic cappuccino is made with an espresso machine that has a steamer attachment. If a steamer is not available, the hot milk can be whipped in a blender for 1 minute.

    Gently fill each of 4 cups one-third full of espresso and one-third full of hot steamed milk and top with one-third foam.

Serves 4.

OLD-FASHIONED COFFEE SODA

3 cups chilled double-
  strength coffee
1 tablespoon superfine
  sugar
1 cup half-and-half
4 scoops (1 pint) coffee ice
  cream
¾ cup chilled club soda
Sweetened whipped cream
  for garnish
4 maraschino cherries for
  garnish

This is a two-straw drink, something to be shared with your sweetheart after the 2 o'clock matinee or with your favorite group of late-night revelers.

Combine the coffee and sugar in a large pitcher. Blend in the half-and-half. Fill 4 soda glasses halfway with the coffee mixture.
   Add a scoop of ice cream to each glass. Fill to the top with soda. Add a dollop of whipped cream and top each glass with a maraschino cherry.

Serves 4.

CIUDAD COOLER

4 cups extra-strength
  Mexican coffee
2 cinnamon sticks
4 whole cloves
3 whole allspice
Cracked ice
½ cup heavy (whipping)
  cream

After a summer stroll through the exquisite shops in the *Zona Rosa* section of Mexico City, nothing can take the place of the cool privacy of your posada's enclosed patio and the refreshing, subtly sweet flavor of this iced coffee drink.

Combine the coffee with the cinnamon, cloves, and allspice in a large teapot or pitcher. Steep for 30 minutes.
   Fill 4 tall glasses with cracked ice. Pour ⅛ cup cream into each glass. Strain the coffee mixture and pour equally into each glass.

Serves 4.

VARIATION: For a low-calorie summer drink, omit the cream and pour the coffee over cracked ice.

Left to right: Old-Fashioned Coffee Soda; Ciudad Cooler; Calypso Cooler (recipe on page 54).

TURKISH COLA FLOAT

2 cups chilled extra-
   strength coffee
2 cups (1 pint) dark coffee
   ice cream
2 cups (16 ounces) cola
Orange slices for garnish

Here's a stimulating refreshment! With its combination of cola and coffee beans, it could be called a Caffeine Cooler, and it may be the perfect solution to an all-nighter.

Fill each of 4 glasses with ½ cup coffee. Scoop ½ cup of ice cream into each glass and top with ½ cup cola. Before serving, decorate each glass with an orange slice.

Serves 4.

CAPPUCCINO BORGIA MILKSHAKE

¼ peeled orange
¼ cup espresso, at room
   temperature
1½ cups chocolate ice
   cream
6 tablespoons freshly
   squeezed orange juice
¼ cup whole milk
Whipped cream for
   garnish
Grated orange zest for
   garnish
Chocolate mocca beans for
   garnish (see page 93)

Jim Roberts runs the best coffee shop in the Northwest, and he knows every conceivable way to combine coffee into a great-tasting drink. This is one of Jim's originals and a favorite of mine. If you're not an espresso lover, it also can be made with double-strength coffee.

Coarsely chop the orange and combine it with the espresso, ice cream, orange juice, and milk in a blender. Blend until just smooth.
   Pour into 2 tall, frosted milkshake glasses and garnish with the whipped cream, orange zest, and chocolate mocca beans.

Serves 2.

Left to right: Turkish Cola Float; Cappuccino Borgia Milkshake; Angostura Cooler (recipe on page 54).

CALYPSO COOLER
(Pictured on page 51.)

1 cup chilled extra-
   strength coffee
2 small ripe bananas, sliced
2 cups (1 pint) coffee ice
   cream
2 to 4 tablespoons rum
Ground cinnamon for
   garnish

Bananas acquire a more sophisticated persona in this delectable drink.

Place the coffee and bananas in a blender. Cover and blend until the bananas are pureed. Add the coffee ice cream and rum. Blend at high speed until thick. Pour into 4 tall, chilled glasses. Sprinkle each cooler with cinnamon and serve.

Serves 4.

ANGOSTURA COOLER
(Pictured on page 53.)

2 cups chilled extra-
   strength coffee
2 cups (1 pint) vanilla or
   chocolate ice cream
1 tablespoon Angostura
   bitters
Whipped cream for
   garnish
Chocolate curls for garnish

The addition of Angostura, an aromatic bitters based on a secret formula of vegetable flavorings created by an English army surgeon in 1830, gives this coffee shake a worldly twist and a refreshing sharpness.

Combine the coffee, ice cream, and bitters in a blender. Cover and blend until smooth.
   To serve, pour into 4 tall, chilled glasses and top with the whipped cream and chocolate curls.

Serves 4.

SCHMIDTY'S IRISH COFFEE
(Pictured on page 57.)

This coffee classic is best enjoyed in front of a warm fire.

Place 2 teaspoons of the sugar and 2 tablespoons of the whiskey in each of 4 warm glass mugs. Fill each mug two-thirds full with the coffee. Top each mug with whipped cream. Do not mix. Savor the warm beverage through the cool layer of cream.

Serves 4.

8 teaspoons granulated
   sugar
8 tablespoons Irish
   whiskey
2⅓ cups hot French-roast
   coffee
Heavy cream, lightly
   whipped

SUPREME BEAN GROG
(Pictured on page 58.)

This is a great drink to fix during the holiday season. The spice base can be made several days ahead and stored in the refrigerator for unexpected visitors.

Combine the spices in a small bowl and mix well.

In a mixing bowl beat the butter until light and add sugar slowly until well blended. Add the spices and mix well.

Place 1 tablespoon of the spice base into each of 4 cups or mugs. Pour 3 tablespoons of light rum and 2 tablespoons of the half-and-half into each cup. Fill each cup with hot coffee and sprinkle the top with orange zest.

Serves 4.

⅛ teaspoon ground
   cinnamon
⅛ teaspoon ground allspice
⅛ teaspoon ground
   nutmeg
⅛ teaspoon ground cloves
2 tablespoons butter, at
   room temperature
2 cups packed brown sugar
¾ cup light rum
½ cup half-and-half
2 cups hot Italian-roast
   coffee
Grated orange zest for
   garnish

CAFÉ ALEXANDER FRAPPÉ

2 cups chilled double-
strength coffee
3 tablespoons granulated
sugar
¼ cup heavy (whipping)
cream
¼ cup brandy
¼ cup crème de cacao
6 ice cubes
Freshly grated nutmeg for
garnish

This might be the very drink you need after a long night at the opera.

Combine all the ingredients, except the nutmeg, in a blender. Cover and blend until frothy.

To serve, pour into 4 glasses and dust the top of each drink with nutmeg.

Serves 4.

CAFFÈ ZABAGLIONE

4 egg yolks
¼ cup granulated sugar
⅛ teaspoon salt
¼ cup dry Marsala wine
¾ cup Italian-roast coffee,
at room temperature

This Sicilian coffee drink is based on the most famous of all Italian desserts. Be sure to serve it immediately after preparing, because the mixture will tend to separate if it is allowed to stand.

Whisk the egg yolks, sugar, and salt in a bowl until they are pale yellow and creamy. Slowly stir the wine into the mixture. Pour the liquid into the top pot of a double boiler. Cook over simmering water and whisk until the mixture becomes a thick foam and soft mounds form, about 5 to 10 minutes. Slowly fold the coffee into the egg mixture until blended. Pour into goblets and serve with a spoon.

Serves 4.

Left to right: Café Alexander Frappé; Caffè Zabaglione; Schmidty's Irish Coffee (recipe on page 55).

NEW ORLEANS COFFEE EGGNOG

Sipped by early colonists, this American original takes on a new identity with a coffee made famous in New Orleans. The addition of chicory root gives New Orleans—style coffee its rich, peppery taste.

You can purchase New Orleans blends in many supermarkets and specialty grocery stores, or in Vietnamese neighborhood markets.

Combine the egg yolks in a large bowl and beat with a wire whisk until thick and pale yellow. Gradually add the sugar to the yolks. Blend in the coffee and ⅓ cup cream. Add the bourbon and let the mixture rest for 30 minutes.

Beat the egg whites in a bowl until stiff. In a separate bowl, whip the remaining heavy cream until soft peaks form. Alternately fold the egg whites and whipped cream into the coffee mixture. Pour it into glasses and top with a dash of freshly grated nutmeg.

Serves 6 to 8.

8 eggs, separated
1 cup superfine sugar
¾ cup double-strength New Orleans—style coffee, at room temperature
¾ cup heavy (whipping) cream
¾ cup bourbon
Freshly grated nutmeg for garnish

ROYALE COFFEE PUNCH

Bob Yule is a track star I used to follow around when I was in pigtails. Now he and his lovely wife Jennifer roast and blend some of the finest coffees available in Redwood City, California. This recipe and the grog on page 55 are two of their favorites when entertaining a crowd.

Combine the coffee, sugar, and brandy in a large pitcher and chill.

Pour the champagne in a punch bowl and add the chilled coffee mixture. Mix gently.

To serve, ladle the punch into champagne flutes or punch cups.

Fills 12 champagne flutes or 20 punch cups.

4 cups extra-strength coffee, at room temperature
2 tablespoons powdered sugar
1 cup brandy
1 fifth champagne, chilled

Left to right: New Orleans Coffee Eggnog; Royale Coffee Punch; Supreme Bean Grog (recipe on page 55).

SAMBUCA MOSCA

Rumor has it that an odd number of beans floating on top of a glass of Sambuca Mosca means success in life while an even number means just another drink.

4 ounces Sambuca
12 to 16 roasted coffee
 beans

Fill each of 4 liqueur glasses with 1 ounce of Sambuca. Float either 3 or 4 coffee beans on top. Light the surface with a match. Serve with the blue flame still glowing. Blow out gently and sip.

Serves 4.

KAFFÉ CARDAMOM

This celebrated after-dinner drink has a sweet, aromatic hint of cardamom. Reminiscent of ginger, but less pungent, cardamom has become the quintessential Nordic spice and is used in baking and in other Scandinavian recipes.

4 cardamom pods, cracked
 and seeded
¼ cup cognac
2 tablespoons curaçao
4 sugar cubes
2 cups extra-strength
 coffee

Combine the cardamom seeds, cognac, curaçao, and sugar in a chafing dish. Heat gently until the mixture is hot. Set aflame for 10 seconds. Add the coffee to the mixture and heat thoroughly. Pour into demitasse cups and savor the taste and bouquet.

Serves 4.

Two liqueur glasses of Sambuca Mosca and a cup of Kaffé Cardamom.

SHRIMP WITH COFFEE MOLE

30 large prawns (about 2
    pounds), shelled and
    deveined
2 bottles beer
1 teaspoon red pepper
    flakes
3 ounces dried mild pasilla
    chili pods
1 ounce dried New Mexico
    chili pods
2 cups hot double-strength
    coffee
1½ tablespoons ground
    coffee
1½ teaspoons ground
    cinnamon
1 tablespoon dried oregano
6 whole allspice
6 whole cloves
1 teaspoon dried thyme
2 tablespoons grated bitter
    chocolate
1 tablespoon vegetable oil
1 large onion, chopped
4 large garlic cloves,
    minced
½ cup golden raisins
3 medium ripe tomatoes,
    cut in half
¼ cup cashews
½ cup blanched almonds
Ripe honeydew melon
    wedges for garnish
Fresh mint for garnish

For seafood lovers. Artist Larry Kirkland adds coffee to this spicy Mexican sauce traditionally used on poultry.

Place the prawns, beer, and pepper flakes in a non-metallic bowl. Cover and marinate in the refrigerator for several hours.

Preheat oven to 300° F. Using kitchen shears, cut the stems off the chili pods. Open the pods, take out any of the white veins, and reserve the seeds. Place the cleaned pods on a baking sheet and warm in a oven for 5 minutes. (Watch the pods carefully so they don't scorch.) Soak the warmed chili pods in 1½ cups hot coffee for 20 minutes.

In a dry frying pan, toast the chili seeds over medium heat for 3 to 5 minutes, shaking the pan to brown the seeds evenly. Place the toasted seeds, ground coffee, spices, and chocolate into a spice grinder or blender and process until all the pieces are finely ground. Reserve.

Heat the oil in a skillet and sauté the chopped onion and garlic for 5 minutes until translucent. Soak the raisins in the remaining ½ cup coffee for 10 minutes. Drain and reserve coffee. Place halved tomatoes, cut side down, on a foil-lined baking sheet and broil 6 inches from the heat until the tomato skins bubble slightly and blacken.

In a food processor, whirl the cashews and almonds until finely ground. Add the onions, garlic, tomatoes, and raisins. Drain and coarsely chop the reserved chili pods and place in processor. Process thoroughly. Add the coffee-spice mixture and process until combined. This is your *mole*. (The *mole* should be moist and thick, resembling oatmeal in texture. Add reserved coffee, a tablespoon at a time, if too dry.)

Place the *mole* in a large enamel pot and bring to boil over medium heat. Simmer for 5 minutes, stirring the bottom constantly to keep from scorching the *mole*.

Drain the prawns from the marinade. Place the prawns in the *mole* sauce and cook over medium heat for 7 minutes, or until just pink and coated with sauce. To serve, place 3 prawns on each plate. Accompany with a small bowl of the warmed *mole* and melon wedges. Garnish with mint.

Serves 10 as an appetizer, 4 as a main dish.

HIDDEN TREASURE FLANK STEAK

2 flank steaks, 2 pounds each
½ cup dried currants
1 cup hot extra-strength coffee
2 cups beef broth
½ cup mild soy sauce
2 tablespoons Worcestershire sauce
⅓ cup honey
1½ teaspoons ground cinnamon
½ teaspoon cayenne pepper
½ teaspoon ground nutmeg
½ teaspoon ground allspice
3 garlic cloves, crushed
2 tablespoons freshly minced ginger
4 tablespoons chopped candied ginger
Blanched carrot strips for garnish
Watercress for garnish

When internationally known Northwest sculptor Larry Kirkland creates a new dish, he thinks about interesting combinations of flavor and texture. These tasty steak pinwheels are a testament to his culinary skills and coffee's subtle charms.

Place the steaks in the freezer for 15 minutes to chill the meat for easier slicing.

Soak the currants in ½ cup coffee for 30 minutes. Drain and reserve the currants.

Place the broth in a saucepan and reduce over high heat by half. Add the remaining ½ cup coffee, soy sauce, Worcestershire sauce, honey, spices, crushed garlic, and minced ginger and continue to boil until your marinade is reduced by half again. (This should make approximately 1 cup of thick and sweetly spicy marinade. Add more honey to taste, if desired.)

Slice the chilled flank steaks across the narrow part of the meat (across the grain) using a long, sharp knife. The slices should be very thin, about ⅛ inch thick. (Your butcher could do this.) If your slices are a little too thick, flatten them with your hand to the desired thinness.

Place the slices in a shallow pan and coat with the marinade. Cover and refrigerate for 2 hours or more.

To assemble, roll each strip into a tight roll, 1½ inches across for an appetizer and 3 inches across for a main dish. As you roll, insert the currants and candied ginger inside the layers of meat.

Place the steak rolls on a foil-lined baking sheet and broil for 7 to 10 minutes, depending upon the thickness of the steak. Serve on a bed of blanched carrots and garnish with watercress.

Serves 12 as an appetizer, 6 as a main dish.

SWEET POTATOES À L'ORANGE

3 medium sweet potatoes,
  peeled
4 medium oranges
¼ cup extra-strength
  coffee
2 tablespoons unsalted
  butter
½ cup chopped blanched
  almonds
2 tablespoons dark rum
1 teaspoon baking powder
¼ cup brown sugar
¼ teaspoon ground
  cinnamon
2 tablespoons grated
  orange zest
Salt and pepper to taste
Fresh mint sprigs for
  garnish
Slivered blanched almonds
  for garnish

Thank goodness the noted botanist, George Washington Carver, liked sweet potatoes as much as he did peanuts. In the late nineteenth century it was Carver who introduced Southern cooks to the many ways of preparing this delicious tuber. In this recipe, I combine the earthy flavors of potato, coffee, and cinnamon with the sweetness of oranges to create an appetizing as well as decorative side dish.

Cut the sweet potatoes into ½-inch pieces and drop into a pot of boiling salted water. Cook until just tender, about 15 minutes.

Meanwhile, cut the oranges in half and scoop out the fruit. Discard the pulp and juice (or save for other uses). Set the orange shells aside.

Remove the cooked potatoes from the heat, drain, and put through a ricer or place in a bowl and mash with a potato masher. Place the mashed potatoes in a warmed bowl.

Add the coffee, butter, almonds, rum, baking powder, sugar, cinnamon, and orange zest to the potatoes and mix thoroughly. Salt and pepper to taste.

To serve, mound the sweet potato mixture in the 8 orange shells. Garnish each filled shell with a sprig of mint and blanched almonds. Serve at once.

Serves 8.

VARIATION: If you are short on time, substitute a 16-ounce can of sweet potatoes. Also, ½ cup chopped walnuts can be substituted for the almonds, and ½ cup raisins, soaked in ½ cup coffee for 30 minutes and then drained, can be combined with the sweet potato mixture.

MADRAS CHILI

In the never-ending search for the perfect chili recipe, I have found one that uses coffee to enhance its spicy richness. I like to serve this chili with hot-from-the-oven corn sticks and ice-cold beer.

In a mixing bowl, cover the red beans with ¾ cup coffee. Soak overnight.

In a deep casserole, heat 1 tablespoon of the oil and sauté the onion and garlic over medium heat until soft, about 10 minutes. Set them to one side, add the remaining tablespoon of oil, and brown the steak cubes.

Add the remaining ¼ cup coffee, spices, and tomatoes to the casserole. Bring to a boil, stir well, and allow to simmer for 10 minutes. Add the beef broth and the drained beans to the casserole and bring to a boil over medium heat. Reduce the heat and simmer for 1 hour. Season with salt.

To serve, ladle the chili into individual bowls and top with the sour cream, grated cheese, and sprigs of cilantro.

Serves 4 to 6.

1 cup dried red beans
1 cup extra-strength coffee
2 tablespoons vegetable oil
½ cup chopped onion
3 cloves garlic, finely
   chopped
2 pounds top sirloin steak,
   cut into ½-inch cubes
1½ tablespoons chili
   powder
1 teaspoon dried oregano
1 teaspoon dried thyme
1 teaspoon ground cumin
1 teaspoon freshly ground
   pepper
1 can (14½ ounces) tomato
   puree or crushed peeled
   tomatoes
1 cup beef broth
Salt to taste
Sour cream for garnish
Grated Monterey jack
   cheese for garnish
Cilantro sprigs for garnish

CAPE GOOD HOPE LAMB KABOB

2 large garlic cloves,
  minced
1 teaspoon salt
2 tablespoons freshly
  squeezed lemon juice
2 tablespoons olive oil
½ cup double-strength
  coffee
2 tablespoons red wine
1½ teaspoons dried
  rosemary
½ teaspoon freshly ground
  pepper
1½ pounds boneless lamb,
  cut into 2-inch chunks
Pineapple wedges
Red pepper wedges
Yellow and red cherry
  tomatoes
Bermuda onion wedges
Fresh rosemary sprigs for
  garnish

The marinade for these lamb kabobs was adapted from a South African recipe in which coffee grounds are rubbed into meat before grilling. Kabobs make a perfect summer meal accompanied with a wheatberry pilaf, mixed green salad, and a fresh peach pie with ginger ice cream for dessert.

In a mixing bowl, mash the garlic and salt into a paste. Whisk in the lemon juice, olive oil, coffee, red wine, rosemary, and pepper. Toss the lamb chunks in the marinade. Cover the bowl and allow the meat to marinate for several hours or overnight in the refrigerator.

Remove the lamb from the marinade and set the liquid aside for basting. Alternate the lamb, pineapple, red pepper, cherry tomatoes, and onion wedges on skewers. Grill the lamb over hot coals for 12 to 15 minutes, basting with the reserved marinade and turning frequently. Serve on a shallow bed of fresh rosemary.

Serves 6.

VARIATION: If you wish to broil the kabobs instead of grilling, place the skewers 4 inches from the heat source and broil for 15 minutes, or until done. Be sure to turn the skewers frequently and baste with the reserved marinade.

CHICKEN BREASTS WITH APRICOT-COFFEE GLAZE

⅓ cup espresso, at room
    temperature
1 cup apricot jam, heated
    and strained
⅓ cup dry sherry
2 teaspoons fresh lime juice
2 teaspoons corn oil
1 teaspoon salt
2 large chicken breasts
    (4 half breasts)

SOUR CREAM SAUCE
1 cup sour cream
1 tablespoon apricot jam,
    heated
4 tablespoons chopped
    fresh cilantro leaves
2 teaspoons grated orange
    zest

Orange wedges for garnish
Fresh cilantro sprigs for
    garnish

Barbecued chicken infused with a sweet apricot and espresso flavor is perfect for a late-summer's-evening grill. The cool tartness of the sour cream and the sweetness of the apricot jam play off each other and create a delicious sauce.

In a mixing bowl, blend the espresso, jam, sherry, lime juice, corn oil, and salt.

Lay the chicken breasts down in a 9-inch-square baking dish. Pour the marinade over the breasts and turn them several times to coat. Cover the dish with plastic wrap and refrigerate 4 hours, turning the breasts several times. Remove the breasts from the dish and reserve the marinade.

Place the chicken on a barbecue grill about 6 inches above a solid bed of low-glowing coals. Cook, turning lightly and brushing with marinade, for 35 to 40 minutes until the breasts are browned on all sides and no longer pink when slashed in thickest part.

To make the Sour Cream Sauce, combine the sour cream, apricot jam, cilantro leaves, and orange zest and stir until well blended. Divide the mixture into 4 small bowls and garnish each bowl with an orange wedge and a cilantro sprig.

Place each chicken breast on a plate and serve with a bowl of sauce.

Serves 4.

ROAD'S END COFFEE CAKE

Easy to prepare, this moist coffee cake is one I often bring when visiting friends for the weekend. It can be made a day ahead, warmed slightly, and then dusted with powdered sugar just before serving.

Preheat oven to 350° F.

In a large mixing bowl, whisk the butter and sugar together. Beat in the eggs 1 at a time until well blended. Stir in 1 tablespoon coffee and vanilla.

Mix together the flour, baking powder, baking soda, and salt. Add the flour mixture to the butter mixture, alternating with the sour cream, until well blended.

Combine the brown sugar, hazelnuts, and nutmeg in a small bowl.

Spread one half of the batter into the bottom of a greased bundt pan. Sprinkle with one half of the hazelnut mixture. Pour the remaining batter on top. Sprinkle with the remaining hazelnut mixture. Bake for 50 minutes. Cool for 15 minutes before removing from pan.

Make Coffee Glaze by mixing all the ingredients together in a small bowl. Drizzle over the cake while still warm. Let the cake stand for 15 minutes to absorb glaze. Dust with powdered sugar and finely ground coffee just before serving.

Serves 8 to 10.

VARIATION: Omit the hazelnuts and nutmeg and substitute ⅓ cup chopped walnuts and 1 teaspoon ground cinnamon. Proceed as directed.

½ cup unsalted butter, at room temperature
1 cup granulated sugar
2 eggs
1 tablespoon double-strength coffee
1 teaspoon vanilla extract
1¾ cups all-purpose flour, sifted
2 teaspoons baking powder
1 teaspoon baking soda
½ teaspoon salt
1 cup sour cream
⅓ cup light brown sugar
⅓ cup chopped toasted hazelnuts (see page 79)
½ teaspoon ground nutmeg

COFFEE GLAZE
1 cup powdered sugar
3 tablespoons double-strength coffee
½ teaspoon half-and-half
¼ teaspoon vanilla extract

Sifted powdered sugar
Pinch of finely ground coffee (Turkish grind)

COEUR CHARMANT

COFFEE CREAM
¼ teaspoon unflavored
  gelatin
1 tablespoon brandy
¾ cup ricotta cheese, at
  room temperature
¼ cup granulated sugar
1 tablespoon finely ground
  coffee (Turkish grind)
1 tablespoon hazelnut
  spread

LAVENDER CREAM
¼ teaspoon unflavored
  gelatin
1 tablespoon Triple Sec
¾ cup ricotta cheese, at
  room temperature
¼ cup minus 1 tablespoon
  granulated sugar
1 teaspoon grated lime zest
1 teaspoon grated orange
  zest
1 teaspoon grated lemon
  zest
1 tablespoon fresh
  lavender florets

CRÈME CHANTILLY
½ cup heavy (whipping)
  cream, chilled
¼ cup powdered sugar
½ teaspoon vanilla extract

Lavender florets for
  garnish
Grated orange zest for
  garnish

This is one of my favorite summertime desserts. It is easy to prepare and the flavors of coffee and lavender are intriguing. But don't omit this dessert from your menu in the winter. Just leave out the lavender and you'll have an orange-scented cream. Serve these tasty hearts as a spread with crisp wafers.

Lightly wipe or spray oil into four ½-cup heart-shaped molds. Set aside.

To make the Coffee Cream, soften the gelatin in the brandy for 15 minutes. Microwave for 15 seconds or heat gently in small saucepan until dissolved.

Combine all the ingredients in a mixing bowl and stir until thoroughly blended. Divide the coffee cream mixture evenly among the 4 heart molds, filling half of each heart mold.

To make the Lavender Cream, soften the gelatin in the Triple Sec for 15 minutes. Microwave for 15 seconds or heat gently in small saucepan until dissolved.

Combine all the ingredients in a mixing bowl and stir until thoroughly blended. Fill the remaining half of each heart mold with the lavender cream. Cover and chill overnight.

To make the Crème Chantilly, pour the cream into a small mixing bowl and whip until the cream leaves a light track on the surface when the beater is raised. Sift in the sugar, add the vanilla, and fold them into the cream. Chill until ready to use.

To serve, place ¼ cup Crème Chantilly on each of 4 dessert plates. To unmold each heart, run a thin knife between the cheese and the mold. Place the mold in a shallow bowl of hot water for 15 seconds. Carefully invert each heart on a wide spatula and slip onto the center of each dessert plate.

Sprinkle with florets and orange zest before serving.

Serves 4.

NOTE: You can find hazelnut spread in most specialty grocery stores. The best-known brand is Nutella. If you cannot find this spread, substitute melted milk chocolate and proceed as directed.

SILVERTON CHOCOLATE CAKE

Virtually all the hazelnuts grown in North America come from the fertile valleys surrounding Silverton, Oregon. Hazelnuts, also known as filberts, have a rich, nutty flavor that complements the bittersweet flavor of semisweet chocolate and espresso. This delicately textured moist cake can be made a day ahead of serving, or eaten the same day it is baked.

Preheat oven to 350° F. Butter the bottom and sides of a 9-inch cake pan lightly. Line the bottom with waxed paper and butter the paper. Set aside.

Combine the espresso, chocolate, instant coffee, and butter in a heavy saucepan over low heat and cook, stirring occasionally, until melted. Set aside to cool.

In a medium mixing bowl, whisk the egg yolks and sugar together until they are pale yellow and fluffy. Slowly stir the chocolate-coffee mixture into the eggs until the batter is well blended.

In a food processor fitted with the steel blade, whirl the nuts for 35 seconds until they form a powder. Add the flour and process for 10 seconds. Measure 1 cup of the chocolate-coffee mixture, turn the processor on again, and add the mixture slowly through its feed tube. Stir the chocolate-coffee-hazelnut paste back into the batter until well blended.

In a large bowl, beat the 4 egg whites with a pinch of salt until they are stiff but not dry and fold them into the batter. Pour the batter into the cake pan and bake for 30 minutes. The center of the cake will be slightly sticky when a toothpick is inserted. Transfer to a wire rack and cool in pan. Unmold the cake onto a platter and sprinkle with powdered sugar and toasted hazelnuts.

Serves 8.

NOTE: To toast hazelnuts and remove their skins, place the nuts on a baking sheet in a preheated 350° F oven for 15 minutes until they turn golden brown. Place the nuts in a terry cloth hand towel. Fold the towel and allow the nuts to "steam" for 5 minutes. Rub the towel firmly between your hands. This will cause most of the skins to flake off.

¾ cup espresso
4 ounces semisweet baking chocolate
2 tablespoons instant coffee granules
6 tablespoons unsalted butter
3 eggs, separated
½ cup granulated sugar
¾ cup raw hazelnuts
6 tablespoons flour
1 egg white
Pinch of salt
Sifted powdered sugar for garnish
Chopped toasted hazelnuts for garnish (see Note)

CUERNAVACA CUSTARD

This velvety version of custard, rich with coffee essence and spices, makes an exquisite dessert for the sophisticated palate.

Preheat oven to 350° F.

In a small, heavy saucepan, combine the water and ¾ cup of the sugar over medium heat. Swirl the mixture until the sugar is dissolved. Bring the mixture to a boil and continue to cook for several minutes until it is caramel in color. Pour the mixture equally into six ½-cup ramekins, coating the sides and bottom of each dish. Set aside.

Combine the coffee, remaining ¾ cup sugar, cinnamon stick, and cloves in a small saucepan. Bring the mixture to a boil, stirring occasionally, and boil for 5 minutes, or until the mixture thickens slightly. Remove from the heat and let it stand and cool to room temperature. Remove the cinnamon and cloves with a slotted spoon.

In a mixing bowl, whisk the eggs, egg yolks, coffee mixture, and liqueur. Gradually blend in the half-and-half and beat until smooth.

Pour the blended mixture into the caramel-lined ramekins. Place the ramekins in a large shallow baking dish containing 1 inch of boiling water. Bake in the lower half of the oven for 25 minutes.

Carefully remove the ramekins from the hot water and let them cool to room temperature. They may be refrigerated for several hours before serving.

To unmold each custard, run a thin knife between the custard and the ramekin and carefully invert on a platter or on individual dessert plates. Serve chilled or at room temperature.

Serves 6.

3 tablespoons water
1½ cups granulated sugar
¾ cup extra-strength coffee
1 cinnamon stick, broken up
2 whole cloves
4 eggs
2 egg yolks
2 tablespoons coffee liqueur
2½ cups half-and-half, heated
Boiling water

COUSIN BETTE'S MOCHA MOUSSE

Bette Sinclair of Portland, Oregon, serves the best frozen mocha dessert I've ever tasted. When I found out how easy it was to prepare, I started fixing it whenever a fast, simple knockout of a dessert was needed. On such occasions, I simply freeze the mousse in a large cut-glass bowl instead of individual soufflé dishes.

Make a collar of waxed paper to wrap around each of six ½-cup straight-sided soufflé dishes. The collar should extend ½ inch above the rim. Secure the edge and bottom of each collar with masking tape. Set aside.

In a small saucepan, mix ¼ cup of the cream and the instant coffee and heat gently until coffee is dissolved. Set aside to cool.

Melt the chocolate chips over very low heat in a small saucepan.

Put the egg yolks and eggs in a blender with the sugar and blend at medium-high speed for 2 minutes. Pour in the cream-coffee mixture, vanilla, and the remaining ¾ cup of heavy cream and blend at medium-high speed for another 30 seconds. Add the melted chocolate chips and Kahlúa and blend until smooth.

Fill each dish equally with the mocha mixture. Carefully place the dishes on a flat surface in the freezer for several hours.

To serve, remove the collar from each dish and press the nuts around the rim of each mousse. Let stand 5 minutes before serving.

Serves 6.

VARIATION: Omit the Kahlúa and substitute another liqueur that complements mocha, such as hazelnut or orange. Proceed as directed.

1 cup heavy (whipping) cream, at room temperature
2 tablespoons instant coffee granules
½ cup semisweet chocolate chips
2 egg yolks
2 eggs
¼ cup granulated sugar
½ teaspoon vanilla extract
2 tablespoons Kahlúa
Chopped pistachios for garnish

BREAD PUDDING WITH COFFEE CREAM

An old-fashioned dessert made even better with the taste of coffee, this is a comfort food for the nineties.

Preheat oven to 350° F.

In a small bowl, combine ½ cup espresso and ¼ cup currants. Set aside for 15 minutes. Chill the remaining espresso.

In another small bowl, combine ¼ cup of the sugar with the cinnamon.

Using 3 tablespoons of the butter, spread one side of each slice of bread and sprinkle with the sugar-cinnamon mixture. Arrange bread, butter side up, on a cookie sheet and lightly toast under the broiler. Cut each slice into 4 triangles. With the remaining 1 tablespoon of butter, grease a 9-inch deep-dish pie plate. Arrange 16 triangles of the bread, butter side up.

In a large bowl, whisk the remaining sugar, eggs, half-and-half, Armagnac, vanilla, lemon zest, and salt. Add the expresso-currant mixture and blend thoroughly. Pour half the mixture over the triangles. Let rest for 10 minutes to absorb liquid. Arrange the remaining 16 triangles of bread, butter side down, on top of the soaked bread. Add the remaining mixture and let stand for 20 minutes.

Set the baking dish in larger pan and add enough hot water in that larger pan to come halfway up the side of the baking dish. Bake in the center of the oven for 45 minutes until custard is set and a knife inserted in the middle of the pudding is withdrawn clean. Cool on a wire rack for 15 minutes.

Meanwhile, to make the coffee cream, combine the cream and remaining espresso in a chilled bowl. Whip the mixture, adding 1 tablespoon of the powdered sugar at a time, until soft peaks form.

Sprinkle the remaining currants over the pudding. Spoon the whipped cream on top or pass separately in a bowl. Serve at room temperature or chilled.

Serves 6.

½ cup plus 2 tablespoons hot espresso
½ cup dried currants
½ cup granulated sugar
1½ teaspoons ground cinnamon
4 tablespoons softened unsalted butter
8 slices homemade white bread, crusts removed
6 large eggs, beaten lightly
1½ cups half-and-half
2 tablespoons Armagnac, or another brandy
½ teaspoon vanilla extract
1½ teaspoons grated lemon zest
¼ teaspoon salt
1 cup heavy (whipping) cream, chilled
2 tablespoons sifted powdered sugar

GRANITA DI CAFFÈ CON PANNA

2 cups water
¼ cup granulated sugar
8 tablespoons finely
   ground espresso-roast
   coffee
1 egg white, stiffly beaten
Sweetened heavy
   (whipping) cream for
   garnish
Chocolate-covered
   espresso beans for
   garnish

Delicious by itself on a hot summer's afternoon or following a spicy evening supper, this traditional Italian dessert ice captures the refreshing tang of espresso coffee beans.

In a saucepan, bring the water and sugar to a boil over medium-high heat. Reduce the heat to low and simmer for 5 minutes. Add the ground coffee to the liquid and steep for 10 minutes. Remove from the heat and filter. Set aside to cool.

Remove the grid from an ice cube tray. Pour the cooled liquid into the tray and carefully place it in the freezer. In 30 minutes, remove the tray from the freezer and stir to break up the ice crystals.

Place the ice crystals in a bowl and blend in the beaten egg white. Return the contents to the tray and return tray to the freezer.

Break up the ice granules every 30 minutes over a period of 3 hours, until the ice acquires a firm, smooth consistency.

To serve, scoop into goblets or champagne glasses. Garnish with lightly sweetened whipped cream and a chocolate-covered espresso bean. For best results, serve the ice the same day you make it.

Serves 6.

COFFEE-ALMOND CRUNCH

Anyone with a passion for nut brittles will love this coffee and almond combination. (I always make an extra batch, but it never seems to last very long.) If you do have any leftovers, you can create a special topping for desserts by pulverizing the almond crunch to a coarse powder in your food processor. You can store it indefinitely in an airtight container and use it at a moment's notice.

2 cups granulated sugar
1 cup corn syrup
½ cup water
1 cup (2 sticks) butter, at room temperature
10 ounces (2 cups) slivered blanched almonds
4 teaspoons instant coffee granules
1 teaspoon baking soda

Generously butter 2 jelly-roll pans.

In a medium saucepan, combine the sugar, corn syrup, water, and butter and melt over medium heat. Cook to 250° F on a candy thermometer, or to the hard-ball stage. Add the almonds and instant coffee and continue to cook to 280° F, or to the soft-crack stage.

Remove the mixture at once from the heat, stir in the baking soda, and mix thoroughly until the syrup foams. Divide it between the greased pans, spreading the hot candy evenly with a metal spoon. When cool, break the slab into pieces and store in an airtight container, unless you eat it all first!

Makes 2 pounds candy.

VARIATION: Omit the almonds and substitute coarsely chopped toasted hazelnuts (see page 79).

MOCHA SLIPPERS

DOUGH
½ cup (1 stick) softened
   butter, cut into chunks
¼ cup granulated sugar
1¼ cups unsifted all-
   purpose flour
3 tablespoons cornstarch

FROSTING
½ cup semisweet chocolate
   chips
1 tablespoon finely ground
   coffee (Turkish grind)

Chopped pistachios for
   garnish

These old-fashioned buttery shortbread cookies are dressed for any
occasion when they are dipped in dark, rich mocha frosting.

In a mixing bowl, combine the butter, sugar, flour, and cornstarch. With your
fingertips or pastry blender, work the mixture until it is crumbly, with no big
lumps. Press the mixture into a large, firm ball. Cover with plastic wrap and
let rest for 15 minutes. Preheat oven to 325° F.
   On a pastry board, roll out dough to ½-inch thickness. With a sharp knife,
cut out desired shapes and place on an ungreased cookie sheet. Bake for 40
minutes, until golden. Cool slightly before lifting from the cookie sheet.
   To make frosting, place the chocolate and finely ground coffee in a small
saucepan over low heat and melt. Blend together with a wooden spoon.
   To frost the cookies, dip the edge of each cookie into the coffee-chocolate
mixture. Sprinkle with nuts and cool on a wire rack.

Makes 1 dozen cookies.

SNOW-CAP COOKIES

½ cup (1 stick) unsalted
   butter
4 ounces unsweetened
   chocolate
4 eggs
2 teaspoons vanilla extract
2 tablespoons instant
   espresso granules
2 cups granulated sugar
2 cups all-purpose flour
2 teaspoons baking powder
½ teaspoon salt
Sifted powdered sugar

**Northwest chef Ron Paul bakes these rich, chewy cookies for his family
and friends. Rolling the cookies in powdered sugar before they are baked
gives each cookie a lacey dusting.**

Melt the butter and chocolate in a small saucepan over low heat.
   In an electric mixing bowl, combine the eggs, vanilla, espresso granules,
and sugar. Beat at high speed until the mixture is very light and fluffy. In a
mixing bowl, sift together the flour, baking powder, and salt. Alternately add
the dry ingredients and the chocolate mixture to the egg mixture. Roll in a
ball and chill the dough until firm. Preheat oven to 350° F.
   Shape the chilled dough into 1-inch balls and roll them in powdered sugar.
Place on an ungreased cookie sheet and bake for 15 minutes. Do not over
bake. Remove the cookies from the cookie sheet and cool on a wire rack.

Makes 3 dozen cookies.

*Left to right: Mocha Slippers; Snow-Cap Cookies; Turkish Velvet (recipe on
page 93).*

COFFEE SAUCE

In a heavy skillet, melt the sugar slowly, stirring often, until the sugar is a light amber color, about 5 minutes. Slowly add 1⅓ cups coffee, stirring constantly. Be prepared for a lot of steam!

In a small bowl, blend the cornstarch and the remaining ¼ cup coffee until smooth. Stir the mixture into the hot coffee-sugar mixture. Continue cooking over low heat and stir until the sauce boils and thickens, about 8 to 10 minutes. Remove from the heat and stir in the butter and salt until blended. Serve warm over ice cream.

Makes 2 cups.

VARIATIONS: To serve this sauce chilled, omit the butter.

1 cup granulated sugar
1⅔ cups extra-strength
   coffee, at room
   temperature
2 tablespoons cornstarch
2 tablespoons unsalted
   butter
⅓ teaspoon salt

TURKISH VELVET
(Pictured on page 91.)

Jim Robert's coffee-rich cookies taste delicious with a cold glass of milk. The coffee bean placed on top of each cookie is actually a candy called mocca, not a chocolate-coated espresso bean. Find mocca beans in any specialty-coffee shop.

Preheat oven to 350° F. Combine the coffee and sugar to make Coffee Sugar.

Sift together the flour, baking soda, and cinnamon and set aside.

In a mixing bowl, cream the butter and sugar until light and fluffy. Add the eggs, espresso, and finely ground coffee and beat well. Gradually add the dry ingredients to this mixture until a smooth dough is formed.

Form a ball from a walnut-sized piece of dough. Roll each ball in the Coffee Sugar and place on a lightly greased cookie sheet. Flatten slightly and press a mocca bean into the center of each flattened ball. Bake for 10 minutes or until cookies rise and crack.

Cool slightly before removing from the cookie sheet.

Makes 2 dozen cookies.

COFFEE SUGAR
½ cup finely ground coffee
   (Turkish grind)
2 cups granulated sugar

DOUGH
3 cups all-purpose flour
1 teaspoon baking soda
2 teaspoons ground
   cinnamon
1¼ cups (2½ sticks) butter,
   at room temperature
2 cups granulated sugar
2 eggs
2 tablespoons double-
   strength espresso
½ cup finely ground coffee
   (Turkish grind)
24 chocolate mocca beans

GENERAL INDEX

Acidity, **14**
Additives, coffee, **23**
Altitude, **11, 14**
American roast, **18**
Antigua, unblended coffee, **14**
Approved Coffee Measure, **27**
arabica, see *Coffea arabica*
Aroma, **14, 17**
Automatic drip coffee makers, **32**

Beans, see Coffee Beans
Body, **15**
Bourbon Santos, unblended
　coffee, **14**
Brazil, **14**
Brewing coffee, **25-27**
　guidelines, **25**
　methods, **28-42**

Caffeine, **12, 18, 20-21**
Celebes, unblended coffee, **15**
Chemex, **32**
Chicory, **23**
City roast, **18**
Clarifying coffee, **42**
Cleaning coffee equipment, **25-26**
Coarse grind, **20**
Coatepec, unblended coffee, **15**
Coban, unblended coffee, **14**
Coffea arabica, **11, 12, 13, 14, 22**
Coffea robusta, **11, 12, 22**
Coffee bean,
　description of, **11**
　freezing of, **19**
　grinding of, **19-20**
　harvesting of, **12**
　raw, **17**
　storing, **18**
Coffee grinders, **19-20**

Coffee grinds, **20**
Coffee plant, **11**
Cold-water concentrate, **28**
Colombia, **14**
Continental roast, **19**
Costa Rica, **14**
Costa Rican, unblended
　coffee, **14, 15**
Countries, **14-15**
Cowboy coffee, **42**
Cultivation, **11**

Dark roast, **19**
Decaffeination, **22-23**
Dominican Republic, **14**
Dry treatment in harvesting, **12**
Dry treatment in roasting, **17**

Ecuador, **14**
Electric grinders, **19, 20**
Espresso, **19, 36, 38**
Espresso grind, **20, 36**
Espresso method, **38**
Ethiopia, **14**
European names for coffee, **13**

Fig, **23**
Filter method, **27**
Filters for coffee brewers, **27**
Fine grind, **20**
Flavor, **15**
Flavored coffee, **23**
Flip-drip method, **30**
French Drip Pot, **30**
French press, **28**
French roast, **13**
Full roast, **17, 18**

Grinding, **19-20**
Grinds, **20-21**

Guatemala, **14**

Haiti, **14**
Hand mill, **19-20**
Harrar, unblended coffee, **13, 14**
Harvesting coffee beans, **12**
Hawaii, **14**
High roast, **19**
History of, **7-9**
Hobo coffee, **42**

Ibrik method, **40**
India, **14**
Indonesia, **15**
Instant coffee, **14, 22, 42**
Italian roast, **13**

Jamaica, **15**
Java, **15**

Kaimaki, **40**
Kenya, **15**
Kona, unblended coffee, **14**

Light roast, **18**

Maracibo, unblended coffee, **15**
Medellín, unblended coffee, **14**
Medium grind, **20**
Medium roast, **18**
Melior, **28**
Melitta, **32**
Mérida, unblended coffee, **15**
Methylene chloride, **22-23**
Mexican coffee, **13, 14, 15**
Mexico, **15**
Mocha, unblended coffee, **15, 40**
Moka Express method, **36**
Mortar and pestle, **19**
Mysore, unblended coffee, **14**

Names of coffee beans
　by country of origin, **13, 14-15**

RECIPE INDEX

by roast, **13, 18-19**
by specialty store, **13**
Napolentan macchinetta, **30**
Neapolitan flip-drip method, **30**

Oaxaca, unblended coffee, **15**
Open-pot method, **42**

Pale roast, **18**
Percolator, **38**
Peru, **15**
Pluma, unblended coffee, **15**
Plunger method, **28**
Pulverized grind, **20**

Roasting coffee, **17-18**
Roasting stages, **17, 18-19**
Robusta, See *Coffea robusta*

Santo Domingo, unblended
coffee, **14**
Spices in coffee, **23, 40**
Sumatra, unblended coffee, **14, 15**
Swiss water-process, **22**

Tanzania, **15**
Tasting terminology, **14-15**
TIP, **8**
Turkish coffee, **20, 40**

Vacuum pot, **34**
Venezuela, **15**
Viennese roast, **13, 17, 18**

Water process decaffeinated
coffee, **22**
Water quality for brewing, **26**
Water temperature for brewing, **26**
Wet treatment in harvesting, **12**
Wet treatment in roasting, **17**

Yemen, **11, 15, 40**

Advice to the Cook, **45**

Beverages (cold):
Angostura Cooler, **54**
Café Alexander Frappé, **56**
Calypso Cooler, **54**
Cappuccino Borgia
Milkshake, **52**
Ciudad Cooler, **50**
Iced Coffee, **49**
New Orleans Coffee Eggnog, **59**
Old-Fashioned Coffee Soda, **50**
Royale Coffee Punch, **59**
Sambuca Mosca, **61**
Turkish Cola Float, **52**

Beverages (hot):
Kaffé Cardamom, **61**
Café au Lait, **47**
Caffè Zabaglione, **56**
Cappuccino, **49**
Espresso, **47**
Schmidty's Irish Coffee, **55**
Supreme Bean Grog, **55**
Vietnamese Coffee, **96**

Cookies:
Mocha Slippers, **90**
Turkish Velvet, **93**
Snow-Cap Cookies, **90**

Desserts:
Bread Pudding with Coffee
Cream, **85**
Coeur Charmant, **76**
Coffee-Almond Crunch, **89**
Coffee Sauce, **93**
Cousin Bette's Mocha
Mousse, **83**

Cuernavaca Custard, **80**
Granita di Caffe con Panna, **86**
Road's End Coffee Cake, **75**
Silverton Chocolate Cake, **79**

Savories:
Chicken Breasts with Apricot-
Coffee Glaze, **72**
Hidden Treasure Flank Steak, **64**
Cape Good Hope Lamb
Kabob, **70**
Madras Chili, **69**
Shrimp with Coffee *Mole*, **62**
Sweet Potatoes à l'Orange, **66**

ACKNOWLEDGMENTS

Thanks go to the friends who generously shared their ideas, time, recipes, and photographic props, especially Larry Kirkland, Jim Roberts, Wanda Ferguson, Jane Foley, Bette Sinclair, Karen Brooks, Ron Paul, Deb Norby, Judd Guitteau, and David Craig. To the businesses who provided props and expertise, especially Coffee Bean International, Coffee People, Starbuck's Coffee, Carl Greve Jewelers, Plate du Jour, and the best espresso cart in Portland, Oregon, stationed outside the Oregon Art Institute. To Shirley Jollymore, my recipe tester, who had the right answers before I even knew what to ask. To food stylist Carol Ladd for her even temper and creativity on and off the set. And to her prop assistant, Nancy Lichtwardt, for her irrepressible energy. To Catherine Gleason, my editor, whose confidence and astute advice were invaluable and whose travel itinerary kept me on my toes. To Ed Gowans, photographer, whose keen eye and gentle nature contributed to another successful collaboration. To production manager and longtime friend Judy Rose, for her ability to bring out the best in each of us and her cheerful reassurance during the late-night hours.

Finally, my thanks go to Bill LeBlond, senior editor at Chronicle Books, for his imagination, trust, and patience. Knowing his midday predilection for Vietnamese coffee, I'm dedicating this last recipe to him:

VIETNAMESE COFFEE

⅓ cup sweetened condensed milk, at room temperature
3 tablespoons medium-fine French-roast coffee
¾ cup hot water, just off the boil

Pour the condensed milk into a tall glass. Place a stainless steel single-cup coffee filter over a glass. (You can purchase this filter in a gourmet coffee store or Vietnamese grocery.) To brew, take off the filter's lid and screen. Add the ground coffee and replace the screen, tightening its screw.

Pour in a small amount of water. Wait for 20 seconds and loosen the screw slightly. Fill the entire filter basket with water. Cover with its lid, and allow water to seep through the filter. After you remove the filter, either stir the coffee and milk together or drink it black and white. This drink tastes just as delicious chilled.

Serves 1.